What Makes Me Feel This Way?

What Makes

Me Feel This Way?

GROWING UP WITH HUMAN EMOTIONS

by Eda LeShan

illustrated by Lisl Weil

Macmillan Publishing Co., Inc.

New York

For my daughter, Wendy,
who taught me so much about feelings—
with deepest love to the beautiful
young woman she has become

ACKNOWLEDGMENTS: To those who read the manuscript and gave so much helpful guidance and encouragement, my deepest thanks: Dr. Catherine Chilman, Mrs. Joan Fiore, Mrs. Jean Schick Grossman, Mrs. Nan Litvak, Dr. Florence Miale, Mrs. Hilda Pearlman, and Miss Myra Woodruff. I am also very grateful to Mrs. Sonya Roach for typing the manuscript—many times over. And, as in all of my work, my love and gratitude to my husband and most important audience, Dr. Lawrence LeShan.

Contents

Introduction

You have probably heard the silly poem about girls being made of sugar and spice and boys being made of snails and puppy-dog tails. You know that boys and girls are made of many things, but not any of those! All human beings are made of muscle and bones, of blood and skin—and hundreds of other things.

But there is one important part of a person that hasn't been talked about very much until the last few years. We just didn't know very much about it. But we have been learning.

This book is all about your feelings. It is much, much harder to read about feelings than about trains or planes or foreign lands or ice skating. When we showed this book to some children, many of them got the giggles and began jumping around a lot. Most of the children were very interested in learning about their feelings, but they felt shy and embarrassed and that's why they giggled. Many children said, "I want to read the book, but I don't want to talk about it." If you do not want to talk about your feelings, you have every right to this privacy.

We hope that you will find out that many of your feelings are shared by other people. Knowing that often makes us feel better about our feelings. We also hope you will see that each person has his own special kinds of feelings, too, and that this is a good thing, for it is part of what makes us all special and different people.

Most of all we hope this book will help you to understand that all children have all kinds of feelings, and that these are natural and you need not be afraid or ashamed of them.

If you want to talk things over with your friends, or teachers, or parents, that's fine—but if you want to just read this book and think about it all by yourself, that's fine, too.

1 • All Kinds of Feelings

Maybe yesterday you were playing a game with your older sister. Because she's bigger and has had time to learn more, she won and you lost. You probably felt good and mad at her. Or maybe last night you suddenly woke up in the middle of the night and thought you heard funny noises. You lay in bed too scared to move or call anyone. Then this morning, you ran into the kitchen and surprised your mother with a great big hug. You just felt like it, because you love her a lot.

Everybody all over the whole world sometimes feels angry, or frightened, or loving, plus a great many more feelings. That's the special thing we are made of, along with everything else—our feelings.

We have been learning how very important feelings are—how they influence just about everything we do. All people get very confused and mixed up about their feelings sometimes, but you will grow to be a stronger and happier person if you can understand more about your feelings.

KNOWING AND FEELING

Feelings are very special. They are not the same as knowing something. You may *know* that thunder cannot possibly hurt you, but there are times when you *feel* afraid of it. Sometimes knowing facts doesn't change a feeling. It may be a fact that every time Aunt Sue comes to visit, she brings you a present and hugs and kisses you. But somehow, you can't figure out why, you have this funny feeling that she really doesn't like children so much. Feelings are just as important as facts, because they affect our lives just as much as facts, sometimes even more. Everybody tells you that freckles are cute, and it seems to be a fact that most grownups like them. But such facts don't change your feelings at all. You hate freckles, and they make you feel that you are ugly. Feeling ugly bothers you, no matter what facts anybody tells you about freckles!

YOUR MIND AND YOUR BODY ARE ONE

Feelings also affect you physically. When it is time to go to the dentist to have a tooth filled, or when the doctor says he has to give you a shot of penicillin, maybe you get a stomach-ache. Or have you noticed that sometimes before a spelling test your heart seems to be beating faster than usual? Everybody, sooner or later, gets that shaky feeling inside when something exciting is about to happen. Some people call it "butterflies in the belly." You just feel awfully excited and a little weak and dizzy.

Maybe you heard your Mom and Dad having a big argument about something at breakfast, and it made you feel worried and scared, although you weren't sure just why. Suddenly on your way to school you got a headache just out of the blue; you can't figure out any reason, because you're not sick. Worries can cause headaches. One important thing we have been learning more about is the fact that the mind and the body are one thing. You *know* in your mind that your stomach aches, and you *feel* your sadness in your stomach.

For an example, you are sitting in your classroom when suddenly you hear a loud explosion. Then the fire drill siren begins to sound. Maybe you were feeling a little sleepy and bored a minute ago. Suddenly you are wide awake; your heart is beating fast. You know exactly what you must do. You leave your seat very quietly and get in the line at the door, and in a minute you and your class are outside the building. You feel excited and scared and ready to run if necessary. Fortunately it turns out that although something was wrong with the furnace, the firemen have taken care of it and you are safe. Later in the day, you don't know why, but you feel tired, even a little sad.

This is why. Your brain receives signals and sends out messages. The minute you heard that explosion, your brain received the message that you were in danger. Then your brain sent the message to parts of your body to make you physically ready to handle danger. One of the most important places this message went was to the adrenal gland, which increased the supply of adrenalin it put into your blood. Adrenalin makes your body work harder than usual during these moments of danger. Later on, when the danger was gone and the body was getting back to a more normal condition, the tiredness of your body made you feel sad and depressed. Feelings always affect your body and your body always affects your feelings. They are all one.

THE FEELINGS WE HAVE

Feelings influence just about everything we do. They affect the way we think about ourselves and about other people. They affect the way we behave. Understanding our feelings can help us to decide what we want to do about them.

If you look back over the past week, you can probably think of many, many feelings you have had. Maybe you lost your temper when your older brother borrowed your bicycle without asking you. You really yelled at him and told him you wished he'd drop dead. Then you began to feel guilty. You don't *really* feel that way about him most of the time, and you were angry at yourself for talking that way.

Or perhaps you and your best friend had a swimming race and you won. You felt really great because you beat him. Or maybe your mother had some guests one evening—people you had never met before. You felt silly and uncomfortable, you didn't know what to say, and you felt very shy.

Maybe you made a careless mistake in arithmetic at the blackboard, and the teacher made a joke about it. You felt very embarrassed and your face got all red. When you found out that a dog had been run over near where you live, you felt very sad. When you couldn't finish that hard puzzle someone gave you for your birthday, you got so mad you wanted to throw the whole thing away. It made you feel frustrated, not to be able to do it. The other day you noticed the wonderful fall colors of the leaves on the maple tree. You wondered how that happens. You felt curious. You wanted to understand more.

Maybe the day before yesterday your mother had to yell at you four times to get dressed for school. You just couldn't believe it was so late—all you were doing was sitting on your bed imagining all kinds of wonderful adventures. Daydreaming takes us away from what is happening around us, and lets us wander off into our own world. Usually it makes us feel good and refreshed afterward.

Maybe the science teacher brought a snake into the classroom last week. You *knew* it was harmless but you didn't want to touch it. Your friends teased you and you felt cowardly. When you knew the right answer in the geography lesson, you felt very smart. When you realized how mixed up you were about subtraction, you felt very stupid.

FEELINGS COME ALL MIXED UP WITH EACH OTHER

Most of the time all different kinds of feelings are mixed up with each other. When you think that Linda and Carol are making fun of you, you hate them—but you also wish they would be your best friends. When Mother says you have to put on a sweater or you can't go out, you feel mad at her—but you also feel glad that she worries about you. You feel excited and happy about taking your sled up to the highest hill, but you also feel scary about trying it for the first time. Or you wonder about people dying, and you feel curious, but then you feel you wish you could stop wondering because it worries you.

FEELINGS HAPPEN TO EVERYONE

When you have some of these kinds of feelings, you think that maybe you are the only person in the world who gets them. Well, there is not a single kind of feeling that you have that most other people don't have, too. People sometimes feel ashamed of some of their feelings, and they try to keep them a secret. But one thing you can be sure about. All the other children and grownups you know have these same feelings. They are feelings of all human beings, and whether we always like them or not, we are stuck with them!

It is normal and natural for all people of all ages to feel angry, shy, sad, happy, embarrassed, frightened, jealous, sympathetic, brave, and cowardly. It is normal and natural to be curious, to wonder, to feel bored, to lose your temper, to feel guilty afterwards.

BUT EACH PERSON IS DIFFERENT

At the same time, people are also different. While we all have these feelings, some have more of one kind than another. Some people's feelings make them behave one way, while the same feelings will make somebody else behave in an altogether different way. No two people really look exactly alike. Even twins, who may seem to be exactly the same, will each have something that is different about them. The same thing is true of feelings. Each person's feelings are special in some way.

John feels very shy when he meets strangers, and he

tries to hide behind his mother or leave the room as fast as possible. Ethel feels shy, too, but she covers it up. She gets silly and wild and runs around a lot, and sometimes people tell her she's a show-off. But she's really just trying not to show how shy she feels.

Penny gets very angry when grownups tell her what to do. When Daddy tells her she can't stay up to watch a certain TV program that some of her friends are allowed to see, she really yells about it! She stamps her feet, or slams the door, or tells her father he's mean and she doesn't like him.

Bill gets just as angry when his mother says he has to stay home because his cold isn't better yet. He *thinks* a lot of mean thoughts about her, but he doesn't say anything. He goes to his room and just doesn't talk to anyone for a long time.

Jerry feels furious when his teacher tells him he has to write his composition over again because he was careless. He doesn't yell or keep it to himself. He tries to talk his teacher out of the extra work. He smiles at her and jokes about it, promising her he'll be more careful next time.

When the guard at the traffic light yells at Tony for starting to cross before he tells him to, Tony feels funny. He feels that the guard is being unnecessarily loud and mean, but Tony is the kind of person who is so afraid of angry feelings that he doesn't even let himself know he feels them. He just feels sort of trembly and unhappy. By lunchtime, he's got a pain in his stomach and can't eat his lunch. His mind didn't know how angry he was feeling, but his body did.

Each person has feelings in his own special way, and behaves in his own special way. This is partly because we are all born special and different from each other, and partly because, from the time we are babies, we learn different things about feelings from our parents.

In Penny's house, everybody says she's just like her mother, who has quite a temper. Since Penny was very small, she's seen how angry her mother can get and how she can yell, too! But Penny's mother gets over being mad very quickly, and later she laughs about it and apologizes to everybody. When Penny was born, she may already have been the kind of person her mother is. Also, all her life she has seen that nothing terrible happens if you get angry and show how you feel.

From the time Bill was born, he has been a quiet person. He isn't a big talker. He likes to be with one or two people at a time, but he feels uncomfortable trying to be friendly in a crowd. His mother and father are also quiet people who don't show their feelings much. Bill knows they love him, but they just aren't the kind of people who do a lot of hugging and kissing. He knows there are times when his parents get angry, but they just don't express it very much, His father gets a cold look in his eyes and his mother sometimes seems to be gritting her teeth and counting to ten. Bill doesn't want to show how angry he feels, and he doesn't think it would be a good idea. He keeps his feelings to himself and likes to be alone for a while until he cools off.

Jerry has been known as the clown in his family ever since he was a baby. He seems naturally to cover up a lot of his feelings by being funny. When he's scared, he sometimes dances and sings and carries on

as if he didn't have a care in the world. And when
he's angry, he makes up jokes. This is partly because
Jerry was just born that way. And partly because he
learned this was a good way to get around his parents,
who are strict and who are always telling him what to
do. He has discovered that by making his parents
laugh he can tease his way out of doing a lot of things
he doesn't want to do.

2 • When Feelings Are Not Allowed

In Tony's house, certain kinds of feelings aren't allowed. His mother and father were taught by their parents that it is bad to be angry, and that nice people never have such feelings. They are wrong, but that is what they have learned, and that is what they are teaching Tony. When a person has feelings that he is very much ashamed of, and feels he is a bad person because he has them, he sometimes pushes away the whole idea of those feelings. He just won't let them come into his mind. But feelings don't give up that easily. They have to go somewhere. Feelings that have nowhere to go often become bellyaches and headaches and make us feel dizzy or very tired. Sometimes they come out all of a sudden, so fast that we can't do anything about them.

Maybe Tony doesn't know how angry he is at the traffic guard. He just can't let himself think about it. Maybe, instead of getting a stomach-ache, he suddenly hauls off and socks the boy next to him at the lunch table who shoved him a little. His feelings just had to come out somehow. He didn't know he was going to do it until after it happened, and he feels terrible. He has been taught that nice boys don't do such things, and he begins to think he is an awful person.

Tony and his parents are right about feelings, in one way. Feelings *can* make you want to do mean things to other people, and that *is* a bad thing. We don't like people to hurt us, so it is easy to see that other people don't like being hurt either. People could never get along with each other at all if they *always* expressed their feelings in what they did. But what Tony and his parents don't understand is that feelings by themselves are neither good nor bad, just normal. It is what we *do* about our feelings that is important.

Suppose, when the guard yelled at Tony, Tony had turned around and hit the guard because he was angry. That would have been wrong. First of all, even if he lost his temper, the guard was really trying to protect Tony from being hurt. Secondly, hurting other people never helps to solve any problem. But just because Tony is feeling angry, he doesn't have to either hide his feeling, or do something bad. He can feel the feeling but not let it make him behave in a way that he knows would be silly or wrong. If he thinks to himself, "Boy, that man makes me mad when he yells at me!" will anything bad happen? No, it will not. *Thinking thoughts cannot make bad things happen. Only actions can make bad things happen.*

WHEN YOU WERE VERY LITTLE

Little babies have feelings, but they don't have words for those feelings. A baby feels happy when his mother holds him tight and feeds him when he is hungry. It is just a good, warm feeling all over. He can't think, "Now I feel happy," because he hasn't learned any of those words yet. When a baby is wet and needs to have his diaper changed, or when someone puts him in his crib to go to sleep but he doesn't feel sleepy and wants to stay with his Mommy and Daddy, he can get very angry. He feels lonely and sad when he is alone. But he cannot think, "I wish that mean lady would change my diaper—she's making me feel terrible and I'm mad at her." He can't think all that, because he doesn't know any words. He just has a feeling, all over his whole self, that something is wrong. Maybe he cries, or gets red in the face, or kicks his arms and legs.

By the time you were two or three years old, you began to know the words for your feelings. Some of these words made you feel good. You said, "I love you, Grandma," and Grandma gave you a big smile and a hug. Uncle Sam said, "How about a piggyback ride?" and you laughed out loud and said, "I'm having fun!" and that felt very good. The grownup people around you seemed to be very pleased about the good and happy feelings you had.

But you begin to have words for other kinds of feelings, too. One day you said, "I hate Bobby, he always takes my wagon." Grownups didn't seem to like it when you had angry feelings. Maybe your mother or the baby sitter or your Aunt Bea said, "It's not nice to say you hate someone." Maybe when you were still quite little, a baby sister or brother was born, and your whole life changed. All the grownups seemed so happy, and they told you how much you were going to love the new baby, how much fun you would have. It didn't seem that way to you at all. The baby was red and ugly, and cried all the time, and your mother was busy and tired, and people just didn't seem to be paying much attention to you any more. You began to think, "I hate that baby. I'm sorry they brought it home from the hospital. I wish they'd take it back."

Somehow, you just know that people aren't going to like you if you say such things. They will think you are a bad person. You wish you didn't have such thoughts —and you just have no way of knowing, unless your parents tell you, that such feelings happen to all children.

WORDS SEEM MAGICAL

But the worst part of all is that because you are still very small, and this is a terribly hard thing to figure out, you aren't quite sure whether the thoughts you think can make bad things happen. Even though that baby is sometimes a pest, it *is* awfully cute sometimes, and it *does* really belong to you and your family. You *do* want to see it grow up and be your friend. When you think about how much you love the baby, you wonder, "Can those awful things I thought about make bad things happen?" The answer is NO, they cannot. But when you are little, you have this awful feeling that somehow thinking about getting rid of the baby can make it happen.

One of the reasons for this feeling is that when you are learning to talk, words seem very powerful and magical. The first time you said, "No, I won't!" everybody got all excited. Your mother seemed very surprised and very angry. All of a sudden, you found out that words can upset people. Or one day when your grandparents were visiting, you said some new words you had just learned. You thought they were simple, ordinary words, but Grandma got very red and embarrassed, and Daddy said, "Jonathan, those are private words. We don't say them when people are visiting." You wondered how a *word* could get people so excited. Words seemed very powerful.

Sometimes little children feel that they can make good things happen if they say a word over and over again. If you got a sled for Christmas when you were four or five years old, you may have said, "Snow, snow, snow!" over and over again. You thought that maybe you could make the wish happen by saying the word. In the same way, if you were angry at your mother when she spanked you, and you thought, "I don't like you, I wish you'd go away and leave me alone!" you got very scared because maybe your thoughts-in-words could make that happen, too.

That night when you went to bed you began to worry. The house seemed too quiet and dark, and maybe you couldn't hear your mother moving around in the kitchen. You couldn't help but feel, "Maybe my mean thoughts have made her go away." You called your mother and told her you wanted her to stay in your room until you fell asleep. Or maybe you asked her to leave a light on in your room or in the hall, so you would feel safe. Probably you had no idea why you felt so scared and worried—you just had that feeling.

Nobody ever completely gets over the feeling that thoughts can make things happen. Have you ever seen your mother or father say something and then knock on wood? Somebody asks your mother if having your tonsils out has made you healthier and stronger. Your mother says, "So far, it seems to have helped a lot— knock on wood." Then she finds something made out of wood and knocks on it. Do you know why she does that? Because she never really got over that old, childish idea about words. She knows it is a superstition, but she still can't help having a little bit of a feeling that if she says things are going too well maybe something will go wrong. Or maybe you've heard someone ask your father how he liked his new job, and maybe he said, "I'd rather not talk about it yet." Maybe he just loves his new job and thinks it's going to be wonderful, but he feels a little afraid of *talking* about it because maybe something will go wrong. He really knows that's a superstition, but he, too, never really got over having just a little of that old feeling that words are magical.

There is no magic that can make words-about-feelings do anything. The real magic is that as we grow up we learn to control what we do about our feelings.

3 • Controlling Our Feelings

Sometimes we feel discouraged with ourselves. We *want* to behave well, but we just can't control our feelings enough. But we do learn, and we become better at keeping feelings from making us do things we really don't want to do.

When a two-year-old gets very angry because someone takes away his pail and shovel, he can't control himself at all. Usually he bites, because that seems to be his best weapon for expressing his feelings. Slowly but surely, he learns he cannot do this. Grownups punish him or separate him from other children. They do all sorts of things to try to make him remember that no matter how he feels, biting isn't allowed. By the time a child is three or four, he can stop that impulse by himself, and that's quite an accomplishment!

But then there are other impulses. At five, when you get angry at someone, you may feel like hitting him. Over the next few years, you learn to control that feeling—most of the time. Your parents and teachers, and you yourself, try hard to learn to talk things over instead of fighting. Most people never learn this completely, but if they care about other people they keep trying. When a parent gets angry and hits a child, he knows he has lost control of himself, and he usually feels very bad about it. Usually he apologizes later and tries to work things out more reasonably. The wonderful thing about human beings is that they want so much to be kind and patient and sensible. They keep struggling to be better people. That's really all anyone can ask of us—that we keep trying.

It is, however, easier to control a feeling if you understand it. Remember Tony? He couldn't stop himself from hitting his neighbor in the lunchroom, because he didn't even know how angry he was. Most people find out that if they can *think* about how they feel, and even find someone to whom they can talk about how they feel, they can begin to control what they do about their feelings.

When we are in kindergarten and first grade, we go on learning ways to control our feelings without having to feel ashamed of them. Larry had a friend in kindergarten who had the most wonderful flashlight he'd ever seen. One day his friend brought the flashlight to school and left it in his locker. Larry had a feeling of wanting that flashlight more than he'd ever wanted anything in his life. He took the flashlight home, and told his parents that his friend had given it to him. That night his friend's mother called up and asked if Larry had the flashlight. When his father asked him abot it, Larry was frightened and he just couldn't tell his father the truth. But his father seemed to understand. He said, "Sometimes you just can't stop a feeling from making you do something you know is wrong. We have to give the flashlight back, but if you want one so badly, let's figure out a better way to get one. If you save ten cents a week from your allowance, then I'll give you ten cents more each week, until you have enough money to buy one." It was a great relief to learn a better way to manage the feeling that he had to have that flashlight.

In third grade, Anne was very worried about herself. She began to think she was a very stupid person because she didn't understand what the teacher was saying about multiplication. Whenever they had a test to see how much the class had learned, Anne was terribly scared. She had a very strong feeling that the only thing she could do was try to copy the answers from the girl at the next desk. Her fear was so strong that several times she just couldn't stop herself, and she cheated on the test. One day her teacher asked her to stay after school. She said she knew Anne was cheating. Anne began to cry and she blurted out, "I try, but I can't stop myself!" Her teacher looked very thoughtful for a minute. Then she said, "Let's do something about it. I'm going to help you with your multiplication for a few minutes every day while the rest of the class is doing something else. When we have a test, I'm going to have all the children sit further away from each other, so they won't be tempted to cheat. And Anne—all I want to know from the tests is who needs help. Some people have more trouble with math than other people. It's nothing to get so worried about."

THERE ARE REASONS FOR RULES

Sometimes grownups are a nuisance to have around! But they can help children find ways to control their feelings, before children are old enough or strong enough to manage their feelings themselves. Some of the rules that often make children angry are really there for just this reason. Children often feel very excited and impatient and can't think about the dangers of traffic. That's why there are traffic lights and school guards. Children sometimes feel wild and jumpy and have so much energy they don't know what to do with it. That's why there are rules on the playground. Children usually want things so badly that they can't wait, and they take what they want. That's why grownups have rules about sharing and taking turns.

And it isn't only children who have trouble controlling their feelings. Grownups need rules and regulations, too, so we have laws and courts, prisons and governments. When a grownup can't stop himself from doing something that hurts other people, his government—the community in which he lives—has to stop him. When children can't stop themselves from doing something that might hurt themselves or other people, it is up to parents and teachers to stop them.

PUNISHMENTS ARE NOT BECAUSE YOU ARE BAD, BUT BECAUSE YOU ARE YOUNG

The trouble with most punishments is that children often get the idea that being punished means that you are a bad person. Many of our parents and grandparents were raised to believe that they were being punished because they were bad. Feeling that you are a bad person is pretty awful. It really doesn't help at all. Nowadays many parents and teachers want to help you understand that when they scold or punish you it isn't because you are bad, but only because you are young and inexperienced. They want you to learn better ways, and they know they must stop you from doing things that are hurtful, when you can't stop yourself. But we hope you will understand that nobody is all good or all bad, that everybody has all kinds of feelings, and that all children—and all grownups—must just keep trying as hard as they can to find acceptable things to do with their feelings.

4 · The Importance of Feelings

It must begin to sound as though the main thing about feelings is how we control them. That's only true of feelings that could hurt us or others. Many of our feelings are wonderful and the best thing we can do is let them flow freely. When we can respect and enjoy our feelings, it seems to make our lives more exciting and interesting. When we can allow our feelings to tell us about ourselves, we begin to know ourselves better.

LETTING OUR FEELINGS SHOW

From the time Kathy was three years old, she'd always had the feeling that it would be fun to be the best at everything she did. She just seemed to be made that way. She was excitable, and daring, and very wiry and strong. She was the first to climb to the top of the jungle gym, the first in her day camp to learn to swim, the champion of the tennis team in high school. She had a marvelous time, and because she was happy and enjoying herself, she got along very well with other people. It was her nature to feel competitive (to want to win) and she and her parents enjoyed watching her be herself.

Alice was much the same kind of person as Kathy, but when she was very little she got the feeling, especially from her father, that it wasn't ladylike to be so strong and competitive and athletic. He wished that Alice would prefer to play with dolls, and learn to sew, and become a good, quiet student in school. Alice fought very hard against her feelings and tried to be the kind of person her father wanted her to be. When we are little we want so much to please our parents, and we are just too young to feel that we can or should also please ourselves. But Alice was only pretending in her feelings, and this was a great strain on her. It made her feel angry and unhappy. She did not have many friends and she did not seem to be able to concentrate on her schoolwork.

Dennis liked to study, and nothing gave him happier feelings than to sit and listen to music or to take his field glasses into the woods to study all the different kinds of birds. He was a shy person, and he liked to spend a lot of his time imagining things. His dad was disappointed. He had been a famous football player in college, and he'd hoped for a son who would follow in his footsteps. Even though Dennis wished he could please his father, somehow he seemed to know, from the time he was very little, that he couldn't do it. In his own quiet way, he let his mother and father know

that there were some things he could do, and some things he couldn't do. By the time he was in high school, he was even able to say, "Dad, I know I'm a disappointment to you, in some ways, but I can't help being different. It's just the way I am." Dennis became a scientist when he grew up. Because he listened to his own feelings, he's a happy person, and his father is so proud of him that he carries in his wallet newspaper clippings about his son's discoveries.

LISTENING TO OUR FEELINGS

When you are young, it is very hard to listen to your own feelings. But it is very important to try to do so, for your feelings tell you a great deal about the kind of person you are and need to be.

Perhaps you are unhappy and embarrassed because

you feel shy. You wish you could talk to people more easily. But you can't. You like to have one or two friends who mean a lot to you, but you hate being with a lot of people. Maybe you are also ashamed because you are not a good fighter—you want to run when someone teases or tries to hit you. You wish you could be different. There is no reason to be ashamed of being this kind of a person. There are millions of shy grownups who lead wonderful and happy lives! Give in to your feeling, and say to yourself, "That's just the way it is. I'm shy, and I'll have to get along with the way I am." When we accept what we are without shame or worry, we usually begin to *enjoy* what we are.

Kenneth hated himself because he was a worrier. It seemed to him he was afraid of more things than any-one he knew. When he was very young he was afraid of the dark, and he worried about wild animals. When he was a little older he worried that his mother or father might die. In grade school, as he learned about some of the problems of the world, he began to worry about air pollution and atom bombs and war. There were many times when he had fun, of course, but it seemed to him that he worried about things much more than most of the people he knew. He even worried about being a worrier! It made him mad at himself, and he began to dislike being the person he was. Then he had even fewer good times.

Some people do seem to be born worriers. But that need not be a disaster! Some born worriers become people like Louis Pasteur or Jonas Salk, and find cures for terrible diseases. Worriers are often very sensitive people like Abraham Lincoln, who care very deeply about everyone. They wish so much for good things to happen—they seem to wish this harder than other people—and that makes them worriers.

There are plenty of things to worry about. We need to work very hard to make things better for the human race. We really need worriers who care. If Kenneth can like what he is, he can make the most of it. Perhaps he can become a doctor or a minister or a congressman. He can then try to turn his worrying into doing something about the things that are bad or dangerous in our world. If he just gets mad at himself and tries to cover up his feelings—if he pretends not to care—he will never be really happy with himself or other people.

Being oneself is the most important thing for every human being. And feelings help us begin to find out what that self is all about.

Feelings are, in a way, the spice of life. Feelings of loving and hating, of wanting to compete with others, or daydreams of adventures—they all make us get out and *do* things. Being ambitious is a feeling, and it can make a person become president of the United States. Imagining forms and seeing colors inside your head are feelings, and the beginning of being an artist. Compassion is a feeling that makes you want to help other people, and that's why people become nurses and social workers. Curiosity and boldness are feelings, and may lead one to become an astronaut.

Feelings also teach us about things we need to know. There are things we really need to be afraid of, in order to be safe. For example, a baby needs to have a feeling of fear about a hot stove. Some parents get confused and annoyed when they find that a child of four or five may become afraid of going into the water, when that same child at two or three used to love to go to the lake or ocean. What has happened is that that baby has gotten smarter! By the time you are five, you *know* more, and one of the things you know is that it is possible to drown. As we grow up, we may find ways to give up some of our fears. For example, we learn to swim well, so that we don't have to be afraid of drowning. But it's a good thing to be a little afraid, so that we are cautious and don't do dangerous things. It's a good idea to be afraid of heights, so that we don't get too close to the edge of a cliff. It's a good thing to be afraid of being hurt, so that we don't drive too fast in a car.

Our own feelings help us to understand other people, and to like them and get along with them. It is almost impossible to care about other people without

first having feelings yourself. Have you ever seen a very young child laugh when someone is hurt? It may be because he has not yet experienced being hurt himself. When someone has taken away your favorite toy, you know how awful it feels. When you feel like taking someone else's favorite toy, you are more likely to be able to stop yourself, because you know how it feels. The more we experience feelings ourselves, the more we can understand and like other people who have the same feelings we have. In a way, that's what loving is all about—caring about how another person feels because we share the same feelings.

5 • Feelings That Confuse Us

Most of the feelings we have been talking about aren't too hard to understand. If somebody is mean to you, you get angry; if something could hurt you, it is natural to be afraid of it. If you get a beautiful red bicycle for your birthday, it's easy to see why you feel happy!

But many feelings don't seem to make any sense at all. Your mind seems to tell you one thing (all about facts) but your feelings won't change. This kind of thing begins to happen almost as soon as you begin to know you are having feelings, when you are two or three years old.

When Michael was four years old, he became terrified of thunder. No matter what anybody told him, he just couldn't get over it. His father explained all the facts about thunder to him, but it didn't make any difference. His mother held him on her lap when there was a storm, and of course he could see that she wasn't afraid—but that didn't help either.

At the age of ten, George had a terrible fear of riding in an elevator. His hands would begin to sweat, and he would feel dizzy just thinking about it. His grandmother lived in a big apartment building, on the seventeenth floor, and he loved to visit her. But when this fear started, he was so upset and frightened that he could not get into the elevator. His mother and father told him this was foolish nonsense. Did he think Grandma would live in a place where there was anything wrong with the elevator? How could it be dangerous if they rode in it themselves? One time George's father grabbed hold of George and pushed him into the elevator, but when he saw how terribly scared George was, he never did that again. Nobody was more confused than George himself. He knew it was a foolish fear, but that did NOT make it go away.

Where do we get these strange fears, and why doesn't knowing facts help them to go away? It used to be that nobody knew the answer to this question. But now we think we have learned what is happening at such times. Have you ever heard anyone talk about "the unconscious mind"? Have you ever wondered why you dream, and why you dream the strange kinds of dreams you dream? Have you ever heard of Dr. Sigmund Freud?

At a time when probably your grandparents weren't even born yet, a group of European doctors, who were trying very hard to understand about human feelings, discovered that there is a part of our mind and our feelings that we are not very often in touch with. Dr. Freud was a leader of this group of doctors, and he discovered that our dreams and our fears very often are messages from that part of our feelings that we don't know about. He called this our "unconscious mind." Since the time in which he lived, we have been learning more and more about this.

Let's go back to Michael and George and see what this means. Michael's mother became so worried and upset about Michael's fear of thunder that she finally called up the pediatrician, who had known Michael since he was a baby. The doctor told her, "Practically every four-year-old I see is afraid of thunder or some other loud noise. It probably has some special meaning to Michael. Many times it has to do with being afraid of your own feelings or other people's feelings. Ask Michael what the thunder makes him think about. Ask him to describe thunder to you—how he feels about it."

Next time there was a storm, Michael's mother sat in a chair with Michael on her lap, and said, "Michael, tell me a story about the thunder. Tell me what it makes you think of." Michael seemed to like that idea very much. He said, "Thunder is a big, bad man. Thunder is a very dangerous giant. He can roar so loud he might kill somebody, and boy, when he gets

mad at you, you better look out! He's so big and strong, he can take a little boy and crush him in his hand!"

Michael's mother was quite impressed. That was some story! She said, "It must be very scary when someone very big and very strong gets angry." Michael said that was true. His mother said, "I guess Daddy must seem almost like a giant to you, and maybe you're afraid he'll hurt you when he gets angry." Michael was very quiet. He seemed to be thinking hard. "Sometimes when I hear the thunder, I think someone might hurt me."

Michael's mother called the pediatrician that same day. "I think we know what that thunder is all about," she said. "It's Daddy in disguise!"

The next few times when there were storms, Daddy took Michael on his lap, and they talked things over—all kinds of things. They talked about fathers and mothers and children; they talked about feelings. Daddy told Michael stories about when he was a little boy, and sometimes he would get angry and scared if *his* Daddy yelled at him. After a few more storms, Michael didn't seem to be scared any more.

George's fears of going in an elevator seemed to get worse all the time. And it wasn't just that. He seemed to start crying when the least little thing went wrong, and his mother was called to school because he was doing such poor work in almost all his classes. His teacher said, "But what worries me most of all is that George seems so unhappy. He doesn't have any fun learning or playing. I think something is really bothering him."

George's uncle was a psychologist—someone who helps people with their feelings, and he thought he knew just the person for George to see. George was scared to death when his parents took him to Dr. Bauer's office for the first time, but she turned out to be a nice woman with white hair and a soft voice. Her office was full of games and toys, and George found out that it was very easy to talk to Dr. Bauer. He went to see her once a week for quite a long time. They played games and talked. They even sang together once in a while, and sometimes just sat and thought. Dr. Bauer seemed to have a lot of interesting ideas. First of all, she thought George was a wonderful boy, and she seemed so glad to see him each week. She also had the idea that maybe George was more afraid of something else than of elevators. She told George they could just forget about the elevators, and think about George's other feelings.

One day they were playing a game of chess and Dr. Bauer won. George got so mad he threw all the chess pieces on the floor, and then he got scared. He looked at Dr. Bauer to see what she was going to do. All she said was, "For such a quiet boy, George, you sure can get angry!"

On another day Dr. Bauer told George she was going on a short vacation. George began to feel the way he sometimes did in the elevator, all choked up and sick to his stomach. They began to play a dart game. By accident George didn't aim very well, and one of the rubber darts hit Dr. Bauer. Only she didn't seem to think it was an accident. She said, "George, if you're mad at me because I'm going away, why don't you just say so? There is nothing so terrible about being angry."

George found out a lot about himself while he was

seeing Dr. Bauer. He found out that he really wasn't such a quiet, well-behaved boy all the time. Sometimes he got pretty mad about things, but he was afraid to let anyone see how he felt. Dr. Bauer seemed to think that wasn't so unusual or strange. One day she said, "George, I don't think it's elevators that scare you so much, but maybe when you get into a small place like an elevator, you feel as though your feelings are just going to explode all over the place." At first George thought this was a nutty idea—but somehow it made him feel better.

About a week later, he told his older brother to stop coming into his room and bothering him. "If you don't stay out of here when I tell you to stay out, I'm going to lock the door," he shouted. Nothing terrible happened. His brother looked very surprised, but he went away.

One day his mother started talking about George's going away to the camp he had been to the summer before. George got very upset, and said, "I won't go—I hated that place—you can't make me go back there!" Nothing terrible happened. His mother just looked very surprised and said, "How come you never once told us that, George?"

He didn't go to camp that summer because his parents decided that the whole family would take a camping trip together instead. One day George's younger sister took his baseball cards without permission, and left them out in the rain. When George found them the next day, he was so furious that he jumped up and down and yelled, "I'm going to kill you, I hate you, I hate you!" Nothing terrible happened. George's father just said, "Calm down, George. I know how angry you are, and Liz did something that was very wrong. She will have to give you some of her allowance so you can start your collection again, but everybody makes mistakes, and I know Liz is sorry now." George still felt mad at his sister for quite a while, but when he saw how bad she was feeling, he finally forgave her.

George was finding out that he could get angry about things without really exploding or hurting other people. After a while he was surprised to find out that he wasn't so afraid of elevators any more, and he was having a much better time at school.

We know now that though some feelings may seem to be foolish and make no sense at all, they *do* make sense in a certain way. Sometimes these feelings tell us about things that are bothering us. It's kind of hard to figure out exactly what they mean, and we may need help from people who understand about such feelings.

There is one especially strange and interesting feeling that is very hard to figure out. It has to do with those times when, for some reason or other, your con-

scious mind doesn't want you to know that you have a certain feeling—probably because you might be ashamed of the feeling if you knew you had it.

Charles was really very frightened of horses. One summer his parents took him to visit a farm where he met another boy his own age, who was also afraid of horses. When Charles saw the other boy crying as a farmer tried to put him on a horse, Charles felt furious at the other boy. He couldn't understand it, but he hated this boy whom he really didn't know at all.

Charles probably could not let himself realize just how frightened *he* was himself, and this other boy brought his own feelings too close for comfort. We very often get mad at people who are having the same feelings we are having—but haven't let ourselves know we have. Whenever we get a very strong feeling about someone else that doesn't seem to make sense at all, it may be a good idea to ask ourselves, "Is that person telling me something about myself that I don't even know about?"

It is very important to remember that feelings mean altogether different things to different people, and no one can figure out just exactly what he may be afraid of by learning about somebody else.

DREAMS

When we dream, we are also trying to work out our feelings. Dreams are never silly, even if they seem to make no sense at all. Dreaming helps us to solve problems, to work out things that are bothering us. Usually we don't even have to try to figure them out—just dreaming often makes us feel better. But if we are very frightened by our dreams, and if we seem to be waking up very scared after our dreams, then sometimes we may need to get help from grownups, just the way Michael and George did with their fears. One thing we know is that dreaming is very important and very good. It helps us in many ways. Good dreams are nice to think about when we wake up. Sometimes we can even use them as the beginning for making up a story, and that can be fun.

Daydreaming is another way that we work out feelings that bother us. When Sue was about seven years old, she loved to lie on the floor in front of the TV set and let her mind wander. After a while she would hardly notice what was happening on the TV screen. Often she made up stories about what it would be like when she was grown up. She would see herself coming into a room, very beautiful, very sure of herself. She would see herself talking easily to other people, telling other people what to do in a pretty bossy way. Sometimes she would be a teacher, and all the children would have to obey her and do just what she told them to do.

In real life, Sue was not sure of herself at all. She thought she was too fat and ugly. She was afraid to talk to the other children in her class because she was afraid they wouldn't like her. She felt her teacher probably thought she was dumb, because she couldn't remember how to spell even some of the easiest words on the spelling list.

There was nothing wrong with Sue at all. Most boys and girls go through periods of time when they don't

like themselves, and feel they can't do anything right. Every single grownup can remember such times when he was a child. Daydreams help you to feel better about yourself. They can give you more confidence in yourself. They help you get over these bad times, when your feelings hurt too much.

Louis liked to daydream in his classroom. His desk was near the window, and he loved to sit and let his mind wander as he looked at the trees and the sky. His second-grade teacher wasn't very happy about it. She thought Louis ought to be concentrating on his workbook. In fact, she made Louis feel very bad about his daydreaming, but he couldn't seem to stop. One day he decided to write a composition about his daydreaming. It was a story about how brave Louis was—how he saved other people just like Superman. He was the strongest and the wisest man in the world. His mother said, "That's a very important story, especially for a little boy who has four older brothers and three older sisters!" In his daydreams, Louis could forget how much he hated being the youngest and littlest in his family.

THE IMPORTANCE OF BEING ALONE

Daydreams usually happen when we are alone. Whether we are dreaming or not, being alone is very important for our feelings. We need time to sort things out, to think things over. Nowadays, children seem to be busy all the time. Usually they are in school until three o'clock, and after school each day there is some special activity. Little League baseball, the dramatics club, music lessons, religious school, dancing classes—all kinds of special activities can be fun and interesting, but they leave you with very little time to be alone with your own thoughts.

Grownups sometimes forget that while keeping busy may be fine much of the time, there ought to be some breathing spells, too. If you begin to feel tired and irritable, if little things begin to annoy you a lot, if you find it very hard to concentrate while you are in school, maybe you are just too busy. Maybe you need to talk it over with your parents, and tell them you want to have a few hours each day when you can do just as you please, all by yourself. Maybe you like to lie on the floor of your room and listen to records, or maybe you like to draw, or read, or climb rocks in the park, or just sit in a tree, doing nothing at all.

Grownups are beginning to understand that such times are very important. They have been finding out that most people are too busy, busy all the time. They flit from one activity to another, always with other people. When we do this we get out of touch with ourselves, and this gives us unhappy feelings. Many grownups have found out that a person who always has to be doing something with other people never learns to use his own imagination or enjoy his own company. In the long run, enjoying being with oneself is very important.

OPPOSITE FEELINGS AT THE SAME TIME

Allen came into his room and saw at once that his older brother had been fooling around with his electric trains, and had changed the way he had set the tracks. It had been a very complicated design of bridges, highways, and tunnels, and it meant a lot to him. He lost control of himself completely, he was so upset and angry. He screamed at his brother, "I hate you, I hate you, I hate you!" At that moment, that was all he could feel. But the feeling of hating can happen when you love someone very much. That is probably the most confusing thing about feelings. Having opposite feelings at the same time surprises us very much when we are children, because it doesn't seem possible.

One of the problems is that when grownups try to help with this confusion, they sometimes mix you up more than before. For example, mothers often say after they have scolded or spanked you, "I'm very angry at what you did, but I love you all the time." You wonder if she can *really* love you at the very same moment that she's absolutely furious. It seems to you that during those moments when you really feel you hate someone, that's the only feeling you have.

Both are true. At one particular moment, if you are having a very strong feeling, you certainly do not have any other feelings—but it is just for that moment. The other feelings are still there inside of you, and they come back very quickly.

In most situations people have many different feelings about the same things and at the same time. Julia is going to be in the school play on Friday, and she has one of the best parts. Her parents and her two older sisters are coming to see her. She is excited, proud, scared, and happy. She can hardly wait, but she also feels like running away! Fred thinks he's going to absolutely *die* when he has to sing a solo in his church chorus, and he's scared to death that all that will come out of his throat will be a frog's croak. He's so nervous that the music director asks him if he'd like to have someone else take his part—and that makes Fred feel even more unhappy!

We all have mixed feelings about people. You really love Grandma. She's been wonderful to you since you were a tiny baby. You know she adores you, and she can be fun to go to the circus with—but boy, can you ever get mad at her when she begins to nag you about getting a haircut!

There is really nobody that we don't have mixed feelings about. Even best friends get on our nerves sometimes, and parents and teachers make us feel a hundred different feelings. There are moments when we suddenly get a wonderful warm glow, deep inside us, about someone else. The day that Dad carried you two miles down a mountainside when you sprained your ankle. The night that Mom sat up with you for hours when you had a bad dream. The day your teacher told you that your painting was one of the most beautiful she had ever seen.

Then there were those other days. Dad said that if you didn't get that garage cleaned out in the next twenty minutes, you were not going on a picnic with your friend and his family. You were so mad, you thought he was so unfair to spring that punishment on you out of the blue, that for that moment you felt like hitting him. Or the time that Mom said you had to wear that awful dress that Aunt Chris made for you because her feelings would be hurt if you didn't. Nobody seemed to be thinking about *your* feelings, and you hated your mother for not realizing just how terrible you thought you looked in that dress. And as for the day your teacher told you you would have to stay in school to take a test that you missed when you were home sick, well, if she could have known what you were thinking about *her*—!

There is a word for these mixed feelings. The word is *ambivalent*. It means feeling two ways at the same time. It means wanting to go to sleep-away camp, but being afraid you will be too homesick. It means admiring your older brother because he's such a great athlete, and also feeling angry and jealous because he's so much better than you are at so many sports. It means knowing that you love your parents more than any other people in the world, and having days when you just can't stand the sight of them!

Everybody in the world, and at all ages, has ambivalent feelings. This begins to seem normal and sensible when we remember that most people, most experiences, most things, are never all terrible or all perfect, but a little of each. Can you think of a single person you know who doesn't have something good about him? Can you think of a single person you know who has nothing bad about him? Do you have anything that belongs to you that works well all the time? The day at the baseball game with your father was just about as perfect as any day in your life—but the traffic getting there sure made your father mad, and those three frankfurters made you feel pretty awful at bedtime. Your dog is just about the most important thing you have ever owned. Although you don't like to admit it, sometimes you think you love him more than any person, but you hate cleaning up after him when he has an accident, and there are days when you wish you didn't have to take him out. The mean old man who lives down the block yells at children if they come near his house. But one day, when some kids were making fun of him from across the street, you noticed that his eyes got watery and his hand was shaking, and you suddenly realized he was a sad and lonely old man.

That's the way life is. People, experiences, things, all mixed up, made up of a lot of qualities. And ambivalent feelings help us come to understand this.

6 • Feelings That Are Easy to Figure Out

WHEN LIFE WAS VERY DIFFERENT

Let's try to imagine what it must have been like to grow up in America one hundred years ago. Most people lived on farms or in small towns. At that time there were fewer people even in the biggest cities than there are now in small cities. There were no cars, no telephones, no airplanes, no radio, no TV. People usually stayed in one place. Most of the people you saw were your own family or neighbors you'd known all your life. There was no dangerous traffic, people in a town all knew each other, and children were on their own much of the time. Most children had hard work to do in the family. Because there were few machines, most work was done by hand and everyone had to do his share. If you lived on a farm, you cut wood for the fireplace, or fed the animals, or helped your father plow the cornfields. The family all worked together and played together. There was no place to go, except to church and to school.

In those days, most children didn't start going to school until they were seven years old, and many didn't stay in school very long—perhaps just long enough to learn to read and write and do a little arithmetic. Because people had to work so hard to make a living, it was quite common for children to leave school at nine or ten or eleven and to go to work in factories or coal mines, or to go to sea on fishing boats. The children of pioneers who traveled West in covered wagons often didn't go to school at all. In those days, parent didn't spend a great deal of time thinking about how smart their children would be. They taught them the things they needed to know in order to survive. They taught them cooking and sewing and building and carpentry and preserving foods. They taught them how to plant and how to milk a cow, or hunt or fish.

Life at that time was just about as different from ours as it could possibly be. Children were told exactly what to do by their parents, and they did what they were told when they were with grownups. But they had much more freedom when they were away from grownups, when they were off in the fields and woods by themselves. They could have many more adventures. Children were included in all the activities of their town. They went to the markets and the church parties, and all the weddings and funerals. At the same time, they usually understood that grownups were the important people, and that they had to keep quiet and do as they were told.

It must be very hard for you to imagine such times. No skyscrapers, no electricity, almost no place at all where there were big crowds and lots of noise. How different from the world in which you are growing up!

Wherever you live now, there are probably many, many people, lots of noisy traffic, strangers all around, very few places where you can just run and play and be on your own. Your relatives are probably spread all over the country, maybe even all over the world. You hear now about so many problems. So many people with so many factories and industries have polluted the water and the air. The noise, especially near airports, is so bad that it rattles the windows. People often seem to be running, running, running, and everyone is always busy, but it is sometimes very hard to figure out what it's all about.

You don't have as many chores as children did one hundred years ago, because getting the food, clothing, and shelter we need just isn't as hard as it was then. But now people are much more concerned about your schooling. Now it seems that everyone must go to school at least through high school, and everyone keeps telling you that you have to go to college, too. You may not work as much with your hands, and you may not be needed as much as a worker in the family, but you have to study and learn.

If you had been a boy one hundred years ago, and there was nothing you loved more than to read books and learn, you might have been very unhappy. You might have wished more than anything in the world that you could study to become a doctor or teacher or lawyer. But in those days your chances of going to college were very, very slim, and most boys who loved to learn from books, but who had to work with their hands, were very unhappy.

Today, anyone who loves to study can be very happy. Everybody wants him to learn and become a scientist or an engineer. But how about the kind of person who just loves to make things? How about the person who finds out about things through what he does, not through reading books? Today that kind of person can often be unhappy, because nobody really cares if he's a wonderful carpenter or can make vegetables grow. They want him to be a student and a thinker.

THE TIMES YOU LIVE IN

The times you live in have a lot to do with your feelings. It is natural for you to feel bored and frustrated and cooped up, sometimes. You live in a time when

people are too crowded together, when there are too many big buildings, too much noise, when people don't have enough space, enough quiet. It is natural for you to feel frightened, sometimes, when you walk down a strange street. It is natural for you to feel uncomfortable and alone, because you live in a time when people move around, when people don't really know their neighbors, and when nobody seems to stay in one place very long—not long enough to stop feeling strange. It is natural for you to worry a lot about your schoolwork, because you live in a time when grownups seem to be thinking about little else than how to make you smarter.

One of the biggest problems about feelings, when you are in elementary school, is that it is so hard to sit still—and people want you to, so much of the time! Often when you feel angry and restless and fidgety, and can't figure out why you feel that way, it may be that you are right to feel that way. Children have a great deal of energy and it is very hard for them to sit still for more than a few minutes at a time. Many schools are beginning to understand this, but many do not. Sometimes, in trying to understand your feelings, you may come to the conclusion that what is really bothering you is not being able to run and jump and yell enough—and you may be right!

It is natural for you to worry about your life and your future, because you live in a time when there are many wars, when people have invented very danger-ous weapons, and everything is changing very fast.

It is very likely that more children bite their finger-nails, have bad dreams, get stomach-aches, feel nerv-ous, can't sit still, and are afraid than ever before. Children haven't changed. The world has changed, and it is harder to grow up now than it used to be—in some ways, at least.

While there seem to be many dangers and many nuisances and many unpleasant things today, there are also some wonderful changes. When you get the flu, you know you are going to get better. When you play in the summertime, you don't usually have to wonder if there will be enough food for you and your family in the wintertime. If you break your leg, you know the doctor can take a picture of your bones and set your leg straight—and without hurting you too much, since he can give you something to stop the pain.

There were good things and bad things about living one hundred years ago. Few people then were trying to understand a child's feelings, and sometimes children were very unhappy. But nobody expected quite so much from a child's thinking. He didn't have to know as much as people expect you to know, and many children were happier and more comfortable than some of you about going to school.

Each time of growing up is different, and each generation of children knows and feels different things. When you have feelings that seem to surprise you a little, you might try asking yourself, "Does this have anything to do with things that are going on around me?" Very often you will find that there are things about your life that make you feel a certain way, and that you might not have felt that way at all, if those things had been different.

Perry has terrible stomach-aches very often: sometimes before he goes to school in the morning, sometimes before he has to take a test, sometimes when he just thinks about having to go to school for at least eight more years. Perry loves cars and motors, and he never gets a stomach-ache on weekends when he can work at his father's garage and help the mechanics. If Perry had lived one hundred years ago, he wouldn't have had to stay in school for eight more years. His father would have been delighted that Perry wanted to learn his trade. He would have become an apprentice, a learner on the job.

Ellen feels ashamed of herself. She thinks she's very clumsy and she hates playing games or going to gym classes. She's very shy with other people, and she keeps twisting her hair nervously, until she almost has a bald spot in one place. What she loves best of all is going away to a farm camp where she can plant vegetables and take care of baby animals. She also loves to help her mother make their dresses. If she had lived one hundred years ago, she might have been too busy doing things she loved to have time for twisting her hair.

Bill is in the principal's office almost every other day. He makes too much noise and disrupts the class. He can't keep his feet still. He starts fights with the boy at the next desk. Outside of school, nobody likes him. The neighborhood policeman tells him he's going to get into serious trouble. Bill's father hits him with a strap quite often, because Bill doesn't come home to his apartment at the time he's supposed to. The apartment is very small, and Bill has six younger brothers and sisters who annoy him. He is very big for his age, and sometimes he feels as though he's going to jump out of his skin. He feels all hemmed in, like a tiger in a cage. He wishes he could just run away.

Imagine that Bill was born in about 1800, and when he was six years old his parents decided to join a group of farmers who were going from Virginia to Minnesota. He would have been outdoors all the time. He would have had to do so much hard work that in the evening he would just have fallen asleep from exhaustion. He would have had many dangerous and exciting adventures. He would have had to know how to shoot a gun, how to fish, how to help get the horses over a river, how to get the wagons down a mountainside. A perfect life for Bill, who needs to be on the move!

The times we live in just happen to us. Sometimes by understanding what our world is like, we can understand our feelings better. But whatever the world may be like, there are things we can do to make ourselves feel better about the world we live in.

7 · Can We Influence Our Feelings?

Carla was seven years old when she heard about a country in Africa where children were starving. There was a war going on in Biafra and the newspapers and the TV news programs showed terrible pictures of children with swollen bellies, crying. Carla was angry and very frightened. She had bad dreams almost every night, and she kept asking her parents how people could let children be hungry.

Her mother and father told her that it was true there were bad people who made wars and were cruel. But all over the world there were also millions of good people who wanted to help. In Biafra there were ministers and priests, and nurses and doctors, and reporters and airplane pilots, who were working terribly hard to help the children.

Carla's mother and father took her to a special meeting outside the United Nations building where people had come to express their horror over the starving children. People brought big bags and boxes of food, and each person bought a candle, and the money for the candles would go to buy more food.

Carla felt a little better. The next day she and her mother made cookies and then they went around to all the apartments in Carla's building and sold the cookies. They made forty dollars and sent all the money to buy food and medicine for the Biafran children. When we get afraid or upset about real things that are happening, we can help ourselves to feel much better by doing whatever we can to help.

Sometimes we can help ourselves with our feelings. Philip knows that every single time something new happens to him, he gets very nervous and worried for a short time. When he was three, he cried the first two days at nursery school. When he was five, he cried when his mother took him to birthday parties. When he was seven, he was scared to death of going on an airplane—and here he is, nine years old, and going to sleep-away camp for the first time. Is there anything he can do about being the kind of person who needs time to get used to new experiences?

Well, he might ask his parents to take him to visit the camp a few weeks ahead of time, or he might ask the camp director if he could make a date with someone who has been there before. Or he might just say to himself, "Now, you *know* you're going to feel sad and homesick for a few days—that's the way you are, but you always get over it!" Sometimes just accepting a feeling, rather than trying not to have it, is a way of changing it.

Ernie was a very moody person. When he was happy he was really flying high, but there were times when he seemed to get "black moods." Every little thing that happened made him feel worse and worse. After a while he learned something about himself. When one of those gloomy moods began, he found that if he tried to write poetry about how he felt, he could sometimes begin to feel better. Sometimes he found that it didn't really help right away, but by the time he began to pull himself out of it, he had written some great poems—and he was fascinated to read about how glum he had been feeling.

Some people can change their feelings by going to a movie, or eating a hot fudge sundae, or buying a new

puzzle. Some people change their feelings by being alone for a while, while others can change a mood by making a date with some friends, or going ice skating or bowling. Sometimes we just have to learn that we are better off if we just avoid certain things or people. Jan realized that every time she watched a horror movie on TV she had terrible nightmares, so she got smart enough not to watch them any more. David realized that every time he made a Saturday or after-school date with Pete, they ended up having an argument. David would feel that Pete had gotten the best of it, and David would get a headache. He finally decided that maybe, for a while at least, it might be a good idea if they both saw other friends.

It isn't necessary or even wise to try to get rid of sad or angry feelings. Sometimes the best thing to do is just to let yourself *feel your feelings*. That's doing something about feelings—letting them happen, and accepting them.

We can do something about other people's moods, too! There are some days when you just *know* it is not the moment to tell Mother that you lost your watch. There are some days when asking for a bigger allowance might work out just fine, and other days when, if you bring up the subject, your father might make the allowance less than it already is. There are days when you can joke and kid around with a teacher, and other days when you'd better stick strictly to business. Watching how other people are feeling can help you to decide what you should do about your own feelings. Because one thing you have certainly known, as far back as you can remember, is that grownups have feelings too!

8 · Grownups and Their Feelings

PARENTS

If it is hard to figure out your own feelings, it is even harder to understand grownups! They can be very confusing. One reason for this is that what they do sometimes expresses exactly the opposite of what they are feeling. When you were only about two years old and ran out into the middle of a crowded street, your mother probably gave you a spanking and yelled a lot. She *acted* very angry, but what she was *feeling* was a terrible fear that you might have been hurt.

When Wendy was about four years old, she got lost. She and her parents were visiting another couple and their little girl in a different neighborhood, and Wendy and Carol went to the playground. Somehow or other they found themselves locked out of the house when they wanted to come back in, so Wendy thought they ought to go look for her house.

When their parents realized the two little girls weren't downstairs, they were frantic. Within minutes the police cars came, and they began a search that lasted several hours. Their parents were nearly crazy with worry. The only thing they wanted in the whole world was to find Wendy and Carol, but when they saw they were safe and unhurt, they began yelling at them, and scolding, and telling them how they were going to punish them. All Wendy and Carol could see was anger; all their parents were feeling was great relief. That is often the way people relieve their upset feelings.

It is also hard to understand grownups' feelings because, when you are young, you just cannot know all the worries and concerns they have on their minds. You have to grow up yourself before you can figure it all out.

It is always hard for every generation of children to really believe that their parents were once children, too. But they most certainly were, and all the things that happened to them affected them as much as your experiences are now influencing you.

Martha's mother is a very fussy housekeeper. She drives her children crazy telling them to pick up their belongings, hang up their clothes, and fold their towels. That's what she was taught as a child, and because she was a very quiet and sensitive little girl, she did what her mother told her to do. Lauri, on the other hand, thinks her mother doesn't make enough fuss. When Lauri's friends come to visit, she feels embarrassed sometimes. There may be a load of laundry lying on the floor, two days' dirty dishes in the sink, and the beds not made. She's ashamed that her mother isn't a neater housekeeper. Strangely enough, Lauri's mother might have had the same kind of bringing up as Martha's mother did. Only she was a more rebellious person, and she got mad when her mother made her clean her room every few hours. She would mutter under her breath, "Some day, when I have my own house, I'm going to live *my* way!"

Some parents who were raised very strictly act the same way with their children. Other parents, also raised strictly, go to the other extreme, and sometimes let their children do things they shouldn't do. People can have similar experiences but react differently, because they have different personalities. But in one way or another, we are influenced by what happens to us when we are children.

There is one very great difference between most grownups and children that makes it hard for them to understand each other. That is that most grownups don't like a lot of noise and jumping around—and most children do! Often when parents and teachers lose their tempers, it is simply because children are shouting and yelling and jumping around so much. Grownups and children also have trouble understanding each other because they want different things. Parents and teachers worry a great deal about what kind of person you will be when you grow up, while the only time that you are really interested in is *right now*.

Let's think for a minute about the parents of that boy who lived one hundred years ago. What were they like? How did they feel? Well, being parents seemed to them the most natural thing in the world. They never really thought about it, except to be happy when a new baby came, and to try as hard as possible to keep the baby alive and well, which was quite hard in those days. They taught each child the things he needed to know in order to survive. If father and mother worked in a factory, chances were that by the time a child was ten or eleven he would be working beside them. If a child seemed to have an unusually good mind and liked to study, he might be one of the lucky few who went to high school and college, and became a doctor or a lawyer or a teacher. All children were taught to believe the same things their parents and grandparents believed. Because the world was not changing so fast then, it never occurred to those parents that what they were teaching their children wouldn't be enough.

Your parents couldn't be more different from those parents. For one thing, the world has been changing so fast that they know that what their parents believed doesn't often help them to live well. They know that by the time you grow up things will have changed so much that what they believe may not help you at all. They worry a great deal, and they feel that they just have no way of imagining what sort of world it will be when you grow up.

They really aren't very sure what to do about this, and because it worries them, they may try hard to find some new answer that seems to make sense. For many parents, the answer is *education*. They think, "I can't tell what the world will be like, but I have to find some way to make Johnny strong enough. All I can think of to do that, is see that he knows a lot." That is why so many parents seem to think about little else than your schoolwork. Chances are that what you need most to get along, no matter how the world changes, is an understanding of yourself and other people, a good imagination, and good feelings about the person you are. Many people believe that when you have those things you can learn and do anything you have to.

One hundred years ago, parents had no way of knowing how much they could upset their children's feelings. There were no people telling parents how to raise their children. There were no people warning parents that if they made a mistake they could ruin a child's life. Your parents have been deeply influenced by the study of human beings mentioned before. Since the time when Dr. Sigmund Freud began to study people's feelings, thousands of people who work in this field, called psychology, have been giving lectures and writing books, advising parents on the best way to raise their children. Sometimes they have been very,

very helpful. Many parents have learned a great deal about how children feel, and have been able to help their children feel good about themselves.

But this is also very confusing, and most parents get mixed up sometimes. One day they think you will grow up to be a better person if they are very strict. The next day they think they must be very careful not to hurt your feelings. One day they believe in spanking, but the next day they feel very guilty if they spank you. When you seem happy, getting along well with your friends and in school, they think, "I guess we are just lucky." But when you are feeling sad or afraid or angry, they think to themselves, "Oh, we must be doing something terrible."

Parents worry a great deal about helping you grow up well. What they sometimes forget is that they can't be any more perfect than you can, and that growing up can't happen without some problems and difficulties. Human beings can't be perfect, and the experiences of living can't be perfect; but sometimes parents forget that, because so many people have been trying to tell them how to be good parents.

There is something else that is very confusing about parents. The feelings they have about themselves often make them behave in a strange way towards their children. Mrs. Montgomery has a little girl who is seven years old. One day Mrs. Montgomery came to school to see Pat's teacher because Pat was behaving very badly at home. Mrs. Montgomery told the teacher, "I don't know what it is, but that child is driving me wild. I see red every time she gets fresh or doesn't do what I tell her to do." The teacher asked, "What sort of person is Pat?" Her mother answered, "She's very strong-willed and she has a quick temper, a great sense of humor, and she's stubborn as a mule." Then, looking very shocked, Mrs. Montgomery said, "Gee—I could be describing *myself!* I guess the reason I get so shook up is because she's just like me, and I want her to be better!"

Mr. Friedman, who is a lawyer, is a very short, quiet man. He's very gentle and soft-spoken. His son Bobby is already very tall and strong and athletic. Bobby knows he can wind his father right around his little finger. His father seems to be beaming at him all the time. Mr. Friedman told his neighbor on the train, going to work, "That Bobby is the kind of boy I wished I was when I was young!"

Sometimes parents feel very good about having a child who is just like them, and sometimes it worries them. It all depends on how they feel about themselves—whether or not they really like themselves. Some people enjoy having children who are different from themselves, and others find this very difficult. Kay's mother says, "I just can't get used to having a daughter who is such a tomboy. When I was little, my mother made such a lady out of me. I always had to be all dressed up and very polite. Here *I* am with this noisy, tough girl, swaggering around the house in bluejeans, using awful curse words, climbing trees better than her two older brothers! She makes me very uncomfortable!" Sometimes a child is just the way the parent always wished *he* could be, and that can make a parent a little jealous.

Sometimes parents can get very upset about something that is happening to *you*, but the upset is really about something that happened to *them*. Ronnie doesn't really worry too much because he can't fight very well. He doesn't like to fight. He has learned his own special way to handle bullies. He jokes with them, and tries to talk to them, and acts like a clown. Soon they laugh, and everything is OK. But Ronnie's father just can't stand it. He was terribly upset when Ronnie got a sock in the eye one day coming home from school. He insisted that he was going to get boxing gloves and teach Ronnie how to fight. Ronnie thought that was a dumb idea, and he couldn't understand why his father was making such a fuss about it. What he couldn't possibly know—and what his father may not even remember—is that once, when Ronnie's father was a little boy, a big bully beat him up, and *his* father called him a sissy. Ronnie's father never got over the feeling that his father didn't think very much of him.

Candy is in the fifth grade, and some of the girls are beginning to talk about boyfriends and making dates. Candy thinks they are nuts. She thinks it's much more fun just to all be pals, and not start that silly stuff. But Candy is a very pretty girl, and her mother makes a big fuss about that. She's always asking if Candy wants to have a party, and she buys Candy fancy party dresses, and she jokes about how all the boys are in love with Candy. It didn't seem to make any sense, until one day Candy and her mother were looking through a picture album, and there were pictures of Mrs. Saunders when she was about ten or eleven years old. She was very plump and had very curly hair, and she wore braces. Candy's mother looked at the picture and sighed. "Oh, Candy, you're so lucky to be so pretty. You won't miss all the fun I did, because I was such a fat, ugly little girl!" Many times parents feel that they have missed something in their own childhood, and they want very much to give what they think they missed to their own children.

Sometimes it is very hard for parents to change their ideas about a child. Most children, while they are growing up, make up an imaginary world of the people they will know and things they will do when they grow up. They imagine the handsome prince or princess they will marry, and the three perfect and beautiful children they will have. The only trouble is that in such dreams the children are not real children, but more like Barbie dolls! Most parents aren't really prepared for the fact that their children will have very strong personalities of their own and can't be molded into a parent's dream. Sometimes when you think your father is angry at you, or your mother is disappointed, it isn't really you they feel that way about—it's just that nobody could possibly live up to their dreams. Most parents realize this, sooner or later.

Sometimes parents will seem to get very angry about something, when you wish they could be more sympathetic or understanding. Sometimes it may be because they had the same problem when they were little, and they are so anxious to reassure you that they do it in the worst possible way. Let's say you are terribly scared of diving off a board into the swimming pool. You wish your father would say, "I know how you feel, son—just put it off for a while, there's no rush." Instead he comes home every day and says, "Well, did you dive yet?" Every Saturday and Sunday he insists on taking you swimming and tries to force you to dive. You get to hate it more and more, and he gets more stubborn about it every day. You can't understand why it is so important to him. Well, it is possible that something like that happened to him when he was young. Even though he really wishes he could stop himself, something deep inside makes him act the very same way his father acted towards him.

Most children grow up with some feeling that they have disappointed their parents. Your parents were no exception when they were children. It may help you to feel more comfortable about yourself if you can remember that many times when they criticize you it is only because someone, a long time ago, was very critical of them. It really isn't so easy to be a parent. No matter what a person believes he should do to be a good parent, some of those old feelings from child-hood get in the way at times.

There are times when a parent tries to be very understanding, and you wish he would just shut up. Your father says, "I understand, Jed—you are jealous of the baby," or your mother says, "I understand, June—you are really very angry at me, not at that doll." You feel as if they had taken all your clothes off and you had no place to hide! You wish they didn't understand so much. At other times, when you feel just awful, they may not understand at all. Like the time you accidentally broke your older sister's transis-tor radio. You felt absolutely *awful* inside. You would have done anything, if the whole thing had never happened, but they yelled, and said you couldn't watch television for two weeks—as if you really needed any more punishment than your guilty feelings!

There are likely to be times when you will feel that something is really bothering you very much, and that you just can't talk to your parents about it, because they would not understand. Fortunately, we usually know a few people who can understand. Some-times it may be an older sister, or a friend; sometimes it is an aunt or uncle that you feel very close to. Sometimes it can be your pediatrician or the minister at your church or a teacher or the school nurse.

TEACHERS

Teachers are sometimes as hard to understand as parents. They can be very changeable in their moods, and it is hard to know if this will be a good day or a bad one. Just as children can never know all the things that a parent is thinking about, there is no way for you to know what may be happening to your teacher. But very often, when you think a teacher doesn't like you, it really has nothing to do with you. Maybe Mrs. Eaton had an argument with her husband at breakfast. Maybe Mr. Greenberg doesn't have enough money to have his daughter's teeth straightened, and it's on his mind while he's trying to teach you about the American Indians. It is very hard for grownups to be around children all day because of that noise and jumpiness business. It's just a difference between grownups and children. You may think you had a very quiet day in school, but when Miss Washington got home she told her mother, "Oh, I've got such a headache—they were so noisy today!"

Young, new teachers are often very scared of all of you. They want to be good teachers, but they are not at all sure they will know how. They are very much

afraid you won't pay attention, so sometimes they act much more strict than they really feel. Some new teachers are afraid of the principal and the older more experienced teachers. They are afraid they will make a great many mistakes. Some new teachers have all sorts of interesting new ideas and plans. They want to have a wonderful time with you. But because you are children and find it very hard not to get silly and excited unless a teacher is strict, the classroom may get too wild, and the teacher feels he or she can't do all the nice things that were planned.

Many teachers become teachers because they really like children. They enjoyed being children themselves, and they remember how it feels to be a child. They know how to make learning fun, but they are always the grownups and they are always in charge. They are not afraid of children, so they know how to make good rules and regulations. Many teachers just cannot imagine doing anything else but teaching, because they love it.

Some people who become teachers should not have chosen that profession. Sometimes they are people who want to feel very powerful and push other people around. Sometimes they are afraid of being with grownups. Sometimes they became teachers only because their parents wanted them to, or because they felt they could have a safe and secure job for as long as they wanted it. Some people are disappointed in their own talents; they really wanted to be writers or actors or doctors but they weren't quite good enough, and so teaching is not really what they would most like to be doing.

Teachers, just like parents, seem to be comfortable with certain kinds of children and perhaps not with others. Mrs. Morgan always seems to love the noisy, active boys in her class, but she doesn't seem too interested in the quiet girls. Mr. Necci kids around with the girls, and teases them a lot, but he gets very mad at the boys when they get too playful. It is important to remember that when you feel a teacher doesn't like you, it may have nothing to do with the kind of person you are, but just that something has made your teacher uncomfortable with that kind of person.

Every single child who goes to school has teachers he will never forget for his whole lifetime. They are the teachers who made some subject so exciting that you wanted to learn more than ever before. Or they made you feel wonderful about yourself, and very confident that you would grow up to be a fine person. In twelve years of school, most children will have perhaps four or five teachers like that. Then we each have a number of teachers that were great some of the time, and not so great some of the time. We got along fine, and we had a pretty good year, but it wasn't anything really special. Most of us have five or six teachers like that. Then there are those awful years —the teacher just didn't seem to like children at all. The teacher was mean and unfair. The teacher had a terrible temper. Every person is likely to have two or three teachers like that while he is in school.

Most of the time, you can manage to get along. You are a strong enough person to understand that people are all different, and it isn't going to hurt you if, as you are growing up, you learn to get along with many different kinds of people. Once in a great while you may be so desperately unhappy that you will have to ask your parents to help you. But most of us realize after we are grown up that being a teacher is a very hard job, and those really special teachers gave us so much that it more than makes up for some of the unhappy times.

9 • Feelings About Being a Boy or a Girl

Jimmy is eight years old, and he thinks quite a lot about the fact that he was born a boy, not a girl. There are many times when he worries about whether or not his body will be masculine enough when he is grown up. He finds himself comparing his body to other boys' and to his father's.

Jimmy has learned where babies come from, and when he was four years old he saw his mother becoming more and more pregnant with his sister Jody. He can't quite believe some of the things he has heard among his friends or even been told by his parents. Everything about sex and love and babies makes him feel mixed up, curious, excited, embarrassed, and sometimes quite upset. Often when these things come into his head, he tries not to think about them.

Jimmy knows that being a boy includes having very special kinds of feelings—particularly that special, secret feeling that happens sometimes when he is alone, perhaps in bed, and finds it pleasurable to touch himself. He may hear some children joke about masturbation, but he worries about whether it is dangerous or bad. He is too ashamed to ask. Masturbation is normal and not dangerous in any way for boys or girls, when it happens in privacy and does not interfere with all the other natural pleasures and interests of a young person.

Jimmy notices girls quite a lot. He finds himself getting very silly and showing off when there are girls around. There is one girl in his class whom he keeps thinking about, and he wishes he was the tallest boy in the class and the best athlete so she would admire him more than anyone else. He feels curious about girls and daydreams about them—what will happen to them as they grow up, how they will look, what it must be like to kiss a girl. All of these feelings happen simply because he is a boy: a perfectly normal boy, just like all the other boys he knows. All these thoughts and feelings are good. They are part of growing up. There is no feeling that one should be ashamed of, nothing that is dangerous or bad about sexual feelings. Only worrying about them is bad. This is a time of life for learning and growing in every way. If we accept ourselves as growing boys or girls, with all the feelings that will bring, then we can also think about the many, many other things that interest and excite us—baseball, ice skating, studying the stars, practicing with the school orchestra, and studying for that spelling contest that's coming up next week.

It is only when we feel ashamed about our sexual feelings that they seem to interfere with other interests. The best thing that Jimmy can do is understand that everything he is feeling and thinking is normal, and that as he grows, things that seem strange and mysterious to him will all begin to make sense. There's no rush. He's got plenty of time to grow from boyhood to manhood.

Jessica is nine years old and she's in love! Stewart has the lowest voice of any boy in her class, and he's tall and has great big velvety brown eyes. He's the best artist in the school and about four other girls are in love with him, too. Stewart blushes purple when the girls tease him about his deep voice. Jessica thinks she will die if Stewart doesn't send her a valentine this year. She is terribly jealous when Stewart chooses another girl to walk to the lunchroom with, but the day he sat down next to her she felt so shy she couldn't eat her sandwich or think of anything to say.

Often at night she lies in her bed thinking about
Stewart and pretending that they are grown up and
married to each other. She makes up things she would
say and do, how she and Stewart would go on picnics
and to the movies. She has all the same wonders and
feelings when she touches her body that Jimmy has—
and every other boy and girl. But her special wonder,
because she is a girl, is how strange it must be to have
a baby grow inside your body.

Sometimes she looks at her mother, and wonders
what her own body will be like when she is grown up.
Some changes are already beginning to happen and

she feels shy and a little bit scared about all the mysteries of being grown up. When she giggles and whispers with the other girls about falling in love, she feels excited, but she also wonders whether she will like growing into a woman, and she can't understand many of the things she hears. Sometimes she wishes she could stop having some of the thoughts she has. She feels ashamed. Maybe something is the matter with her. Nothing is the matter. She is a normal girl having the same thoughts and feelings as all the other girls she knows. If she can believe that and accept all the experiences of growing, then she, too, can enjoy all the other interesting and exciting things that are part of growing up.

FEELINGS THAT COME LATER

Some of your mixed-up feelings come about simply because you cannot understand the feelings that grownup people have. Sometimes this is because you must wait for your body to grow up. You cannot understand the feelings of being in love, of getting married, having babies, until you are a man or a woman. Sometimes you cannot understand until your mind has grown up, until you have had many experiences and learned a great deal. The best thing to do about such feelings is to say to yourself, "I

just can't tell how I will feel when I am a grownup, so I'm not going to worry about it now." One of the most common subjects that make you feel very confused, and one that sounds either very silly or very awful, is how people have babies. You have probably been taught the *facts*, but you can't understand the *feelings* at all. That is perfectly normal and natural. Let yourself grow, be patient. You will understand the feelings when the right time comes.

One kind of feeling that really upsets a great many children is the idea that you might ever want to leave your parents. You hear them talking about when you go away to college, or when you have your own apartment, or when you get married, and it sounds completely crazy. The last thing in the world that you can imagine is being able to live away from your family. You will understand the feeling of wanting to go out into the world on your own when the right time comes.

There are a great many feelings that worry you about being grown up. You cannot imagine having a job, or being a mother or a father; it sounds dumb or scary. Most of all, you cannot imagine yourself getting so old that you might not have any parents any more. That is the most frightening of all.

Right now, you just cannot take care of yourself. That's what being a child is all about. That's why nature gives newborn creatures, even lions and cows, dogs and ducks, parents to help them grow up. Right now, you know you need to be taken care of. Sometimes it makes you mad, and you wish you could be the boss—but most of the time it is a good, warm feeling to know you will be looked after. There is no way for you to try to guess what it feels like to be grown up. But when you are, you will feel good about being able to take care of yourself and your family. You won't be all alone, then. All your friends will have grown up, too, and you will help each other. Sometimes the best thing to do about a feeling is to tell yourself to wait a while and see how you change.

10 · The Fear of Death and Dying

When you worry about dying, or about the death of other people, you are sharing in a fear that is part of all people of all ages. Death is the great mystery of life, and human beings are the only living creatures that know they will someday die. Your fears are about something that is very real in everyone's life.

Throughout the ages, people have tried to find explanations of death, and ways of comforting themselves. Many people feel they know the meaning of death—others say it remains the great mystery. But somehow or other, every person has to find a way to feel good about his life and to look forward to each day of living, while at the same time knowing that at some time, death does come. It is hard to think about dying, and many times we wish we just didn't know about it. When we are young, our first and biggest fear about dying is that our parents might die and that we would be alone. It is important to remember that we are loved by many, many people, and we will *never* be left alone. We worry and wonder about what death is really like—and many children begin to have fears about going to sleep, because they are not sure if that is in any way like death.

Young children also have a hard time understanding about heaven, if their parents belong to a religion that believes in heaven. When you are little you can only imagine places that you have seen. The idea of heaven is just too big and mysterious. As we get older, religious belief may bring a great many of us help and comfort in accepting the knowledge of death; it has for many thousands of years. But there are other people who need to find other comforting ideas about death.

There are certain things we do know that can help everyone, whether they go to church or not. For one thing, whatever happens to the body when a person dies, the person isn't gone completely. Part of him is alive in his children. Part of him is alive in the good things he did for other people. Part of him is alive in the memories of the people who loved him.

Kim's grandmother died two years ago. Kim misses her terribly. She has a book of pictures of her grandmother, and every once in a while she and her mother bake cookies using Grandma's special recipe. Kim thinks, "When I grow up and have children, I'll teach them the recipe, and they'll teach it to their children, and Grandma will go on and on."

Another thing we know about dying is that it happens when a person is either very, very sick, or very, very old. Sometimes a person may die in an accident, but that does not occur very often. Death is something natural that happens when a body cannot manage to live any more, and things from the outside don't cause that. But young children are often confused about this.

Lennie was six years old when his grandfather died. Grandpa had lived in Lennie's house for quite a while, and he had been sick most of the time. Grandpa needed a great deal of quiet and rest, and people were always telling Lennie to "Shush!" Lennie was a normal little boy, and it was very hard for him to remember not to shout and bang and jump. In fact, it got to be so bad that he began to feel very angry at his grandfather and wish he'd go away so he didn't have to be quiet all the time. When his grandfather died, Lennie was so upset and frightened he couldn't even cry. He had loved his grandfather a lot, and he was sure that his mean thoughts and his making noise had killed his grandfather. This is often the way young children think. Lennie was wrong. His grandfather died because he was a sick old man, with a worn-out heart. There was no one he loved more than noisy, jumpy Lennie, whom he knew was just a normal boy who needed to have fun.

Nobody can ever love another person every single minute. Nobody can be good and quiet all the time. It is perfectly natural to have had angry feelings about a person you also care about a lot. Such feelings have absolutely *nothing* to do with this matter of dying.

Another thing we know about death is that when a person you love dies you need to show how you feel about it. You need to be with all the other people who are also very sad. Sometimes parents have not understood this. They hate to see their children suffer and so sometimes they try to protect their children from seeing them cry. Sometimes parents will send their children to a friend or neighbor's house when a relative dies. In some cases, parents have even kept the death a secret for a long time, because they cannot bear to make their children unhappy. Many parents do not let children go to funerals. They think the children will be too upset at seeing grownup people cry.

We.are learning that children need to share sadness at such times, that they will feel much, much better if they themselves can cry and be comforted by the people they love. It is not just grownups who need to be with each other, and to help each other accept the death of someone they love. Children need that comfort even more, and it is much more frightening and upsetting to be sent away than to see grownups cry. Many parents now believe this.

Another thing we know about growing up and the problem of death is that children are much more scared when they do not know the facts. Sometimes a parent will feel, "I just can't tell my child about how a person is buried in the ground, or cremated in a fire—it sounds too terrible." He may not realize that what a child imagines can be much, much worse than the true facts. The idea of death is a very painful and frightening thing, but as children know quite well, nothing about it is as bad as what we think about when no one will tell us the facts.

When someone dies we need to remind ourselves that there is no reason to be scared of our feelings. It is natural to cry and to feel terrible. It is natural to want to be with your mother and father, and to sit on their laps, and have them hug you a lot. It is natural to feel very funny, and excited, and curious, and strange. It is natural not to be able to believe it,

and to feel sure that tomorrow the person will suddenly come back and it will all be a bad dream. It is natural, sometimes, if this person was someone very, very important to you, to feel almost nothing at all for a while. The shock of the death is just too much to realize all at once, and so for a while a person doesn't feel anything, until he feels strong enough to face it. This is the way grownups feel, and this is the way children feel. When all people let their real feelings come out, they begin to be able to go on with their lives again, as they must.

There are two very important things about death. When someone dies, we realize how precious his life was. We are reminded of the fact that there will never, ever be another person just like this one. Human beings, we realize, are the most important and wonderful things in the whole world, and we feel a deeper love for our family and our friends than we have ever felt before.

Death also reminds us of how precious *life* is—and how much we want to make our lives matter. When someone we love dies, it helps us to bear the pain if we think about what that person would like us to do. When Peggy's grandfather died, Peggy remembered how she and her grandfather had loved to take walks in the country together, and look at the flowers. Grandpa's favorite flowers were pansies. He and Peggy would laugh together about their funny "faces." Peggy decided to plant a little garden of pansies in her back yard. She knew that would have made him happy, and it made her feel good to remember him every time she looked at her little garden. Doing something in memory of a loved person brings that person close to us.

11 · Feelings About Who We Are

OTHER PEOPLE'S PROBLEMS

One thing we have learned about childhood is that no matter who you are, or what you look like, you often wish you were somebody else! All children seem to feel that way. If you have brown eyes, you wish they were blue. If you are the oldest child in your family, you wish you were the youngest. If you are an only child you wish you had brothers and sisters, while some of your friends who have brothers and sisters envy you! If you are a little clumsy and not very good at sports, you wish you could be a good athlete, while your best friend, who is captain of the baseball team, often wishes he was as smart as you are in school.

Have you ever heard a grownup say, "The grass is always greener on the other side of the fence"? That means that things always look better somewhere else than where you are. The reason for that is really very simple. You *know* how it feels to be *you*, and every single person has problems. But you often don't know how another person feels.

Jeff's father is a truck driver, and Jeff has four brothers. They live in a small apartment on a noisy and crowded street. At school Jeff meets Frank, whose father owns a chain of restaurants. Frank lives in a house with a swimming pool and a maid, and he has only one sister. He has a new bicycle, a movie camera, and even a TV set in his own room. Jeff thinks it would be wonderful to be Frank, and have everything he wanted. Frank feels the same way about Jeff. When he visits Jeff's house, Jeffs' mother is always there, and she's always baking cookies and cakes, and the children are allowed to make a mess when they are playing. Jeff's father spends a lot of time playing ball with Jeff and Frank down at the playground in the park. Frank thinks it must be wonderful to have brothers to play with, and a mother and father who are home a lot. His parents both work very hard, and he only really gets to spend a lot of time with them on weekends. Each boy has many good things, and each one has things that aren't so wonderful, but each one thinks that the other has no problems at all.

As far as Sandy can see, her friend Marsha is just a perfect girl. She has long blond hair and a beautiful figure, and she's very good at her schoolwork, always getting A's. Sandy feels very ugly and stupid. She thinks she's too thin, and she hates her straight brown hair, and she's so dumb in the arithmetic class that

sometimes she goes and hides in the girls' bathroom during the class. Oh, if only she could be Marsha! Then she gets to know Marsha better. She finds out that Marsha's parents are divorced, and that Marsha almost never sees her father, who has married someone else and now lives in a city quite far away.

No matter how wonderful somebody may seem, no matter how great their life may look from the outside, everybody has some problems. That's just the way life is. Sometimes we can feel better about who we are, and what our life is like, if we really make the effort to find out about how another person feels.

HOW WE FEEL ABOUT OURSELVES

Why do we all wish we could be somebody else? It isn't just because we often don't know how another person feels. It is partly because when we are very little and love our parents more than anything else in the world, we want to please them, and sometimes we get the idea that we aren't the way our parents want us to be. That is the beginning of wishing we could be somebody else. We are too young to understand, and parents sometimes say things that hurt our feelings. They don't always realize how sensitive we are. A mother may say, "Judy, you can't eat so much candy and cookies—you will get too fat." Right away, Judy thinks, "My mother thinks I'm too fat." Or a father will say, "Tom, there isn't any reason for you to be afraid of the dark—you're too big now." Right away Tom thinks, "My father thinks I'm a sissy and a coward." Judy's mother only meant that too many sweets aren't good for anyone, and that it isn't healthy to gain too much weight. Tom's father didn't realize how he would feel—he was really trying to buck him up and make him feel bigger.

When we are little, it sometimes seems that parents are never satisfied with us. They always want us to be better. They are always saying, "You can do this," or "There's no reason you can't do that." They have forgotten how such things made them feel when they were young. They want you to grow up to be the best and strongest person you can possibly be, and they feel they must do everything possible to correct you, to push you a little into the next stage of growing up. It isn't that they really disapprove of you, it's just that their minds are sometimes too much on what you can be when you are grown up. That seems to be a natural way for parents to be. And it seems to be very natural and normal for children to get the idea that their parents are not satisfied with what they are. That makes a child feel it might be better if he could be like somebody else.

THE WAY THE WORLD TREATS US

Sometimes the way we feel about ourselves has to do with the way we think the outside world feels about us. Some black children have the feeling it would be better to be white. They have learned that many people can be cruel to black children, and that being black in America can often mean that you don't have as good a chance to live in a nice neighborhood, or get a good education, or get the job you want when you are grown up. This is a very real feeling that comes from very real bad things in the world around us. The feeling is a true feeling. But things are beginning to change in America. More and more people are realizing how very bad such a thing is, and

they are trying to change it. Black mothers and fathers and black children are beginning to understand how proud they can be of how hard they have had to struggle to have a good life. Betty can hardly believe that once, a long time ago, her great-great-grandfather was a slave, brought to this country to work in the cotton fields. That was a terrible thing, and she is very proud of her family because they suffered a great deal, but have done wonderful things in spite of it. Betty's grandfather taught himself to read and write, and when he was only fourteen years old he walked all the way from Memphis, Tennessee, to Chicago, Illinois, where he went to work in a factory.

Betty's father worked his way through high school and college and now he and Betty's mother are working very hard to see that black people can have a better chance for a good life. Betty sees that while it isn't easy to be a black person in America, she can really be very proud of her family.

Children who are American Indians, and children whose parents are Japanese Americans and Chinese Americans, often feel the same way. They wish they could be white, because the whole world often seems very mean and cruel to people with red or yellow skin. Slowly but surely, as they grow up and learn more about their own families and about the history of their own people, they begin to realize they can have proud feelings. The world is beginning to change, and millions of people want *all* children to feel good about who they are and who their families are, and want all children to have a good chance to grow up to be whatever they want to be.

Children who feel that the color of their skin makes life harder for them are sometimes very surprised to hear how many white children think the same kinds of thoughts. Jack sometimes wishes his parents weren't Jewish. There is a boy in the neighborhood who calls him bad names and makes fun of him. Once, he went to the Catholic church with a friend of his, and he loved the stained-glass windows, and the music, and the statue of Jesus's mother, looking so tender and full of love.

Leo wishes his parents didn't talk in Italian so much. When his friends visit, he feels embarrassed because his grandmother speaks with such a strong

accent and doesn't look at all like the other grand-
mothers he sees, who seem to be much younger ladies.
His grandmother looks old and wears black dresses all
the time. It makes Adam feel funny to be Polish. His
relatives have funny names that are hard to pro-
nounce, and they talk all the time about "the Old
Country." Gertrude thinks it's terrible that her father
is a shoemaker. She wishes he worked in an office and
wore a suit and a tie, like so many of the other fathers.

When we are young, it is very hard to feel that we
are different from other people. We feel so unsure
about ourselves, and we think that if we could be just
like most of the other people we see, we would feel
stronger and happier.

But as we get older, we begin to understand that
being special can be interesting and even quite wonderful. Jack will be learning about the history of the
Jewish people, and he will begin to realize the
remarkable ways in which the Jews have managed to

survive for so many thousands of years against so many problems.

Even while he is young, Leo begins to realize how much he loves his grandmother, because she tells him funny stories about coming to America, and because she is so full of love. Adam admits he really likes to hear how when Grandpa got off the boat there were thirty relatives he'd never seen before, who came to hug and kiss him. Gertrude begins to find out that her father is one of the best shoemakers in the city, and that the reason he works so hard six days a week, from early morning until late at night, is so that some day she can go to college if she wants to.

As we get older, we like the things that make us special and different. When we are very young, the best thing we can do is know that we have uncomfortable feelings about being different just because we are children, and that they will change when we grow up. There is no reason to feel guilty about our feelings. They are just the way most children feel.

WHEN IT IS HARD TO STAND ALONE

When you are young, it is natural to feel that you want every other person to like you. Sometimes you want this *so much* that you do things you really don't want to do. One day Richard was walking home from school with some of his friends. They were all feeling silly and excited, and one of the boys began throwing pebbles at the basement windows of the houses along the way. Some of the others began to join in, but Richard didn't want to. They teased him and taunted him and said he was "chicken," but even though Richard wanted to be well-liked, he just couldn't do it—so he left them and went home. That takes a great deal of courage, but we learn that in the long run we will feel much happier if we do what *we* feel is right, even if it sometimes means our friends get angry at us for a while. It is very nice to have people like us—but it is even nicer to feel we can like ourselves.

THE THINGS WE CANNOT CHANGE

Sometimes our reasons for wanting to be somebody else have to do with real problems that we cannot change. Leslie was born with one leg shorter than the other, and all she can think about sometimes is how she wishes she could walk and run the way other children do. Every single day, Harry has to have an injection, because he has a disease called diabetes. How he wishes he could be like other people, who don't have to worry about eating candy and ice cream! Paul's father died when he was six years old, and Paul wishes he could be like the boys he knows at school, who can play with their fathers, and talk to them. Lucy's parents are divorced, and her mother cries so often that Lucy is scared and feels terrible and wishes her parents had stayed married to each other.

These are real problems, and nothing can make them go away. There are bound to be times in all our lives when we feel just terrible about such things. We are jealous of other people, and angry at having such "lousy, rotten luck." Such feelings are perfectly natural, and there is no reason we should feel ashamed of them. It *is* very, very hard to have such things happen to us. It is never a child's fault when such things happen. It has nothing to do with being good or bad, naughty or nice. These are things over which children and their parents have no control at all. It helps a lot if we can give in to our bad moods some of the time, and not try to hide our feelings.

But one of the most wonderful things about human beings is that they have the courage to live with pain and disappointment, and to make something good of their lives even under the most difficult circumstances.

Leslie cannot run and jump, but she loves to listen to music. One day she asked her parents if she could take violin lessons. She found out that playing the violin made her happier than anything she had ever done before.

When Harry was nine years old, his parents found out that there was a special camp he could go to where all the children had diabetes, and where the counselors could help him learn to do many of the things other children do. He had the most wonderful time. It made him feel better to see how many other children had to have an injection every day and could not eat candy and ice cream, and he began to see that he could enjoy himself a lot anyway.

One year, Paul went to visit his uncle and aunt for the Christmas holidays. His uncle was a wonderful friend, and told Paul he could come to visit any time he wanted to. It was almost like having a real father.

One day Lucy met a new girl in her school, and found out that Sherry's parents were divorced, too. It helped a lot to have someone she could talk to, who often felt as sad and upset as she did. They comforted each other.

BEING A BOY OR A GIRL

Sometimes what bothers you the most is that if you are a girl, you wish you were a boy, and if you are a boy, you wish you could be a girl. That is also one of the things we cannot change. Irene wishes she were a boy. She has two older sisters, and she's always had the feeling that her mother and father were hoping she'd be a boy. Actually, she is quite a tiny girl, and she loves playing with dolls and making dress-up clothes. She thinks she'd like to be a nurse when she grows up. But Daddy likes to play games, and take long hikes, and work in his shop in the basement, and Irene wishes she could like those things and make her father happy. She often thinks, "If only I'd been a boy, like they wanted me to be!"

Alfred wonders sometimes if it wouldn't have been better if he'd been born a girl. He loves to help his mother with the cooking, and he likes painting much more than going out and playing football. His father calls him a "Mama's boy" and seems very upset whenever Alfred says he wants to cook a whole dinner for the family, all by himself. Even his mother looks worried when he comes home from school and goes into his room to paint, instead of playing outside or riding his bike. He is afraid to tell them that what he would really like to be when he grows up is a great chef in some famous restaurant.

There was a time when it was very natural for children to feel this way. Even today, some grownups still seem to have the idea that boys have to behave one way and girls another, and that girls must only like to do the things their mothers do, and boys only what their fathers do. But all this is changing. By the time you are grown up, you will be able to do anything you want, and still be the same sex you now are. We have learned that a man can be a dancer, a painter, a nurse, a cook, or a fashion designer, and still enjoy being a man and a husband and a father. We have learned that a girl can be an engineer or a doctor or a lawyer or a newspaper reporter, and still enjoy being a woman, a wife and a mother. Most of all, we have learned that the only way to really enjoy being a man or a woman, is to do the thing that makes you feel good about being who and what you are.

When Bernie was six years old he saw a ballet on TV, and it seemed to him it was the most beautiful thing he had ever seen in his whole life. He loved to dance, and he loved to listen to music. He asked his parents if he could take ballet lessons. His father laughed and said, "Not on your life—dancing is for sissies!" Bernie felt awful. He didn't want to be a sissy, but he sure did wish he could some day be part of a beautiful ballet. He began to worry about being a sissy. If he liked to dance, maybe there was something wrong with him. When his father asked him if he'd like to go fishing with him, Bernie pretended he liked going fishing. When his father tried to teach him how to play basketball, Bernie pretended so hard to like playing basketball that he got to be very good at it. When he was on the basketball team in high school it made him feel good to see his father so happy and proud. The only trouble was that he didn't know what he wanted to be when he grew up, and since he was so mixed up, he just did what his father told him to do. He became a salesman, like his father, but he was never very happy.

Danny was very much like Bernie. When he was

seven, his mother took him to see a ballet called *The Nutcracker*, and he thought he had never seen anything so wonderful in his whole life. He asked if he could go to dancing school, and his father said, "Sure—you can try it, if you like. It's very, very hard work to be a good dancer. You have to develop very strong muscles. You have to be a great athlete to be a good dancer." Dan found out that he was built just right to be a dancer. Nothing made him happier than to practice the exercises that would help him to develop the leg and arm muscles he would need for leaping and lifting the girl dancers. He studied dancing all through high school, and went to a special college where he could study dancing. Now he performs in *The Nutcracker*. He is married and has two little girls—and he feels good about being the person he is, because he is doing what he loves best in the whole world.

Being a girl today is different than it used to be. Until quite recently, girls were only allowed to be teachers or secretaries or mothers. When they pushed very hard and demanded the right to be anything else, people thought it was terrible. If a girl said she wanted to be a doctor, she was probably told, "Well, it will be all right if you are a nurse." If she said she wanted to be an airplane pilot, her parents probably said, "Well, it might be all right for you to be an airline stewardess." But we have learned that the most important thing about enjoying being a woman is having the right to be and to do whatever makes you feel best about being yourself. By the time you grow up, it will be quite all right for girls to be explorers and architects and even astronauts.

Caroline loved to read about boats when she was a little girl. When she got older, she loved making her own model boats and sailing them in the lake in the park. She dreamed daydreams all the time about being the captain of a great ocean liner, but everybody told her she was silly—girls couldn't do such things. When she grew up she became a secretary, but she often wished she'd been a boy and could have gone to sea. She was not a very happy person.

Annette was crazy about boats, too. But her parents thought that was just fine. When she was old enough, they sent her to a special camp to learn to sail. While she was at this camp, on Cape Cod, she visited a place called Woods Hole where there is a research center for studying all about the oceans. She talked to people who were studying ocean plants and fish. When she grew up, she went to a special college to study oceanography—all about the seas. Now she is a grown woman and she works in a laboratory, studying what people can do about the pollution in the oceans. She lives near the water, and she and her husband and children go sailing all the time. She loves what she is doing, and she's very glad she was a girl who grew up to be a woman.

THE VERY BEST KIND OF FEELING

The most important feeling in the world is *feeling you are being yourself*. All these years, while you are growing up, you have time to figure out just what that will be. It would be no fun at all if everybody was exactly like everybody else. What a boring world that would be! It will be no fun at all if you try to be somebody that you really don't want to be. How unhappy grownups can be, when they let that happen to themselves! The wonderful thing about being a human person is to find out just exactly what kind of person *you* are, yourself, different and special from all the other people in the world. When you are young, this is very hard. You don't know what kind of person you are, and you are scared to make other people angry. You want to please your parents and teachers, and so you try very hard to be the person you think they want you to be. As you get older and stronger and know more about yourself, you will be able to say, "This is what I want to be. This is what I want to do."

Many of your parents and teachers are beginning

to understand how important this is. We have learned that when a person is most himself, he can be kind to, and thoughtful of, other people. When a person is happy being himself, he can feel love and understanding for other people. When a person is doing his own thing, he wants everybody else to have the same chance, too. People who are happy in what they are doing are able to help other people feel good about themselves, too.

That is why it is a good idea to begin to understand your own feelings. Your feelings help you find out what sort of person you are. Sometimes your feelings hurt; they make you sad and unhappy. Sometimes your feelings fill you with excitement and joy. Sometimes it takes a great deal of courage to think about your feelings. But it is worth it, because all the time that you are learning about feelings, you are learning who you are, and what other people are like. No matter where you live, or what you do, or how much the world changes, that is the most important part of growing up.